Five Popular Persian Ballads

For Solo Classic Guitar • Arranged by Lily Afshar

AF008467

COVER PICTURE © BY CHRISTIE'S IMAGES NEW YORK

© 2000 BY MEL BAY PUBLICATIONS, INC., ALL RIGHTS RESERVED.
WWW.MELBAY.COM

Table of Contents

Gol-e-Gandome (Wheat Flower).. 4

Dareneh-Jaan/Aziz-Joon (Darling Dareneh/Darling Aziz) 6

Leila-Leila.. 10

Jaan-e-Maryam (Darling Maryam).. 12

Lala-ee (Lullaby) 15

About the Author... 16

The five ballads are selected from Persian folk music. They are arranged here in their purest and most direct form. They speak directly to people and although old, they remain popular with Persians to this day. The ballads originate from various parts of Persia where different dialects are used. In these arrangements I have tried to give the melodies the same nuance and embellishments that a singer would. All the ballads except *Dareneh-Jaan/Aziz Joon* begin with a short introduction establishing the tempo and mood. In *Jaan-e-Maryam*, the muted strumming of the melody is an imitation of string tremolo. The arrangement of the *Lala-ee* is inspired by a version for choir by the late Iranian composer, violinist, and conductor, Rouben Gregorian.

The *Five Popular Persian Ballads* have been recorded by Lily Afshar on *A Jug of Wine and Thou*, Summit Records, DCD 236, and performed on Lily's *Virtuoso Guitar* DVD published by Mel Bay.

Gol-e-Gandome

Composed by Lily Afshar

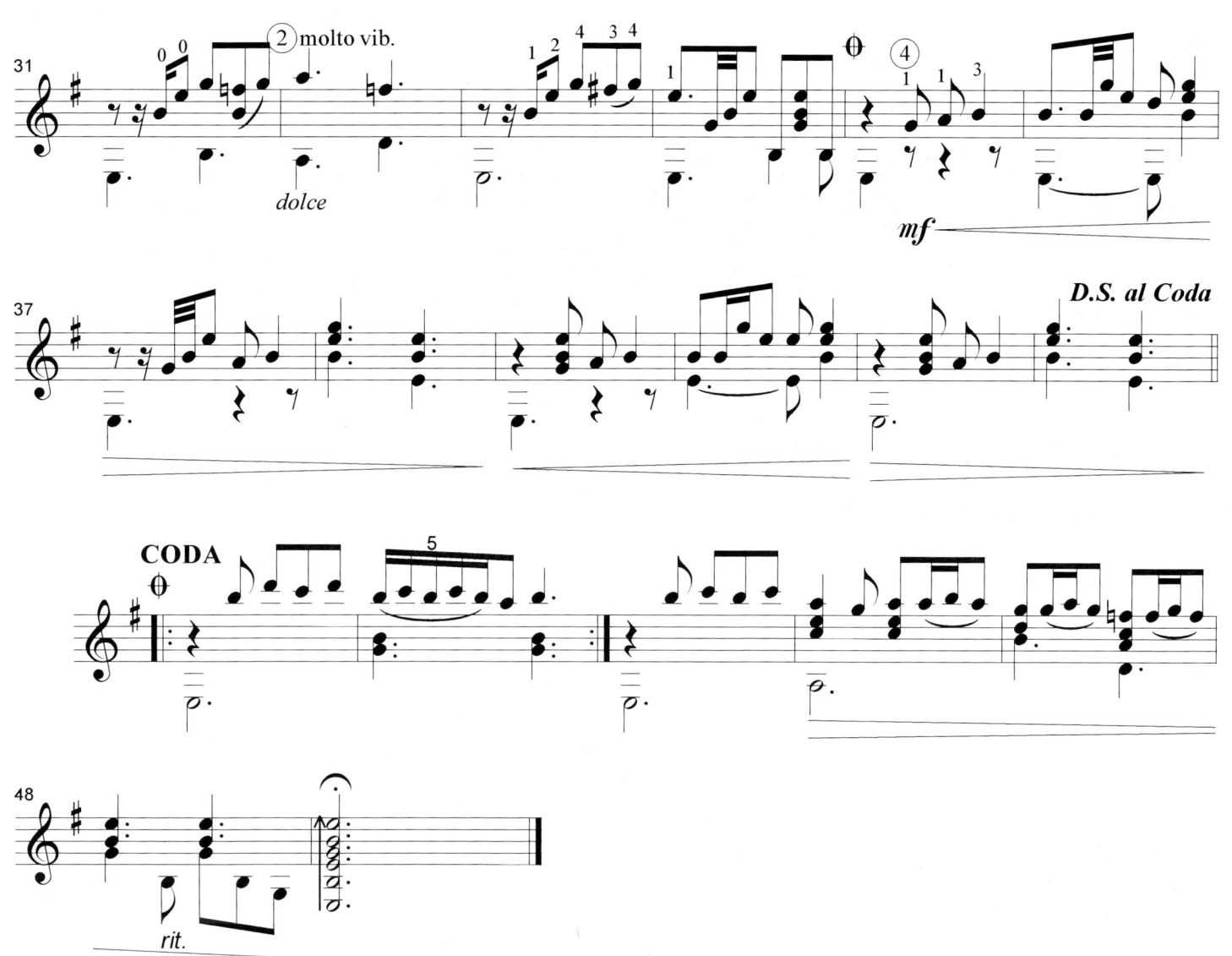

Dareneh Jaan/Aziz Joon

Composed by Lily Afshar

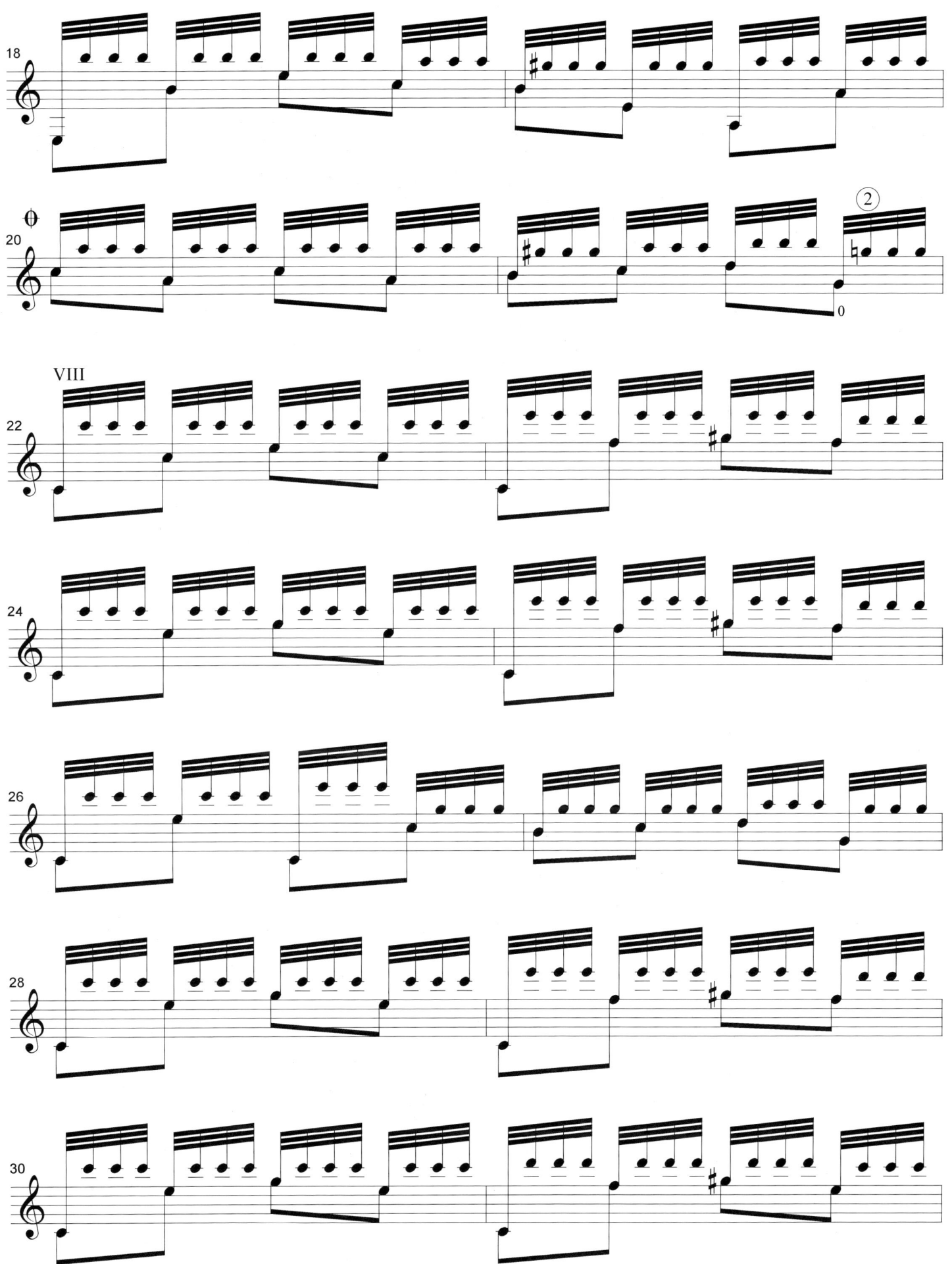

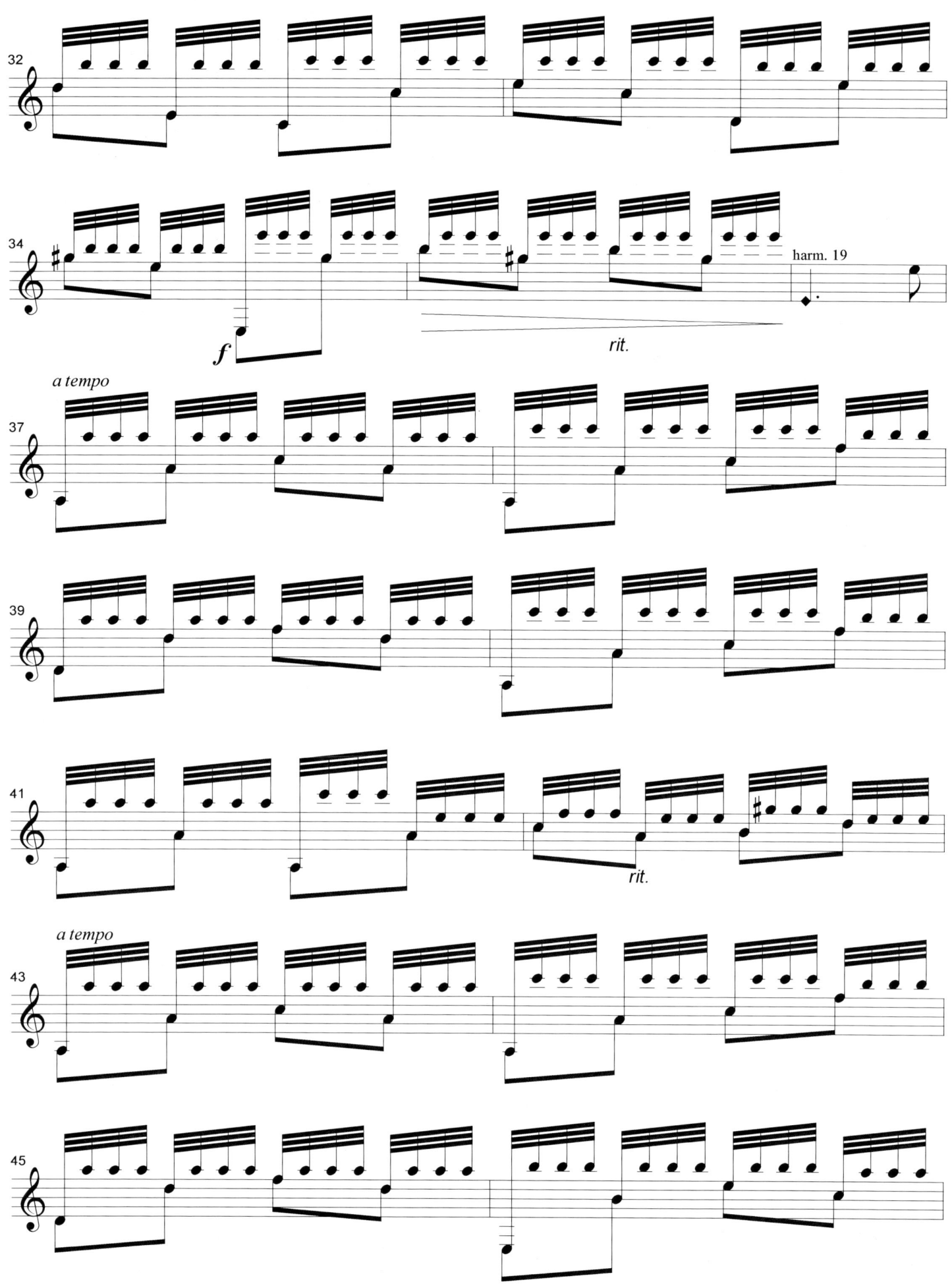

Leila-Leila

Composed by Lily Afshar

Jaan-e-Maryam

Composed by Lily Afshar

Lala-ee
(Lullaby)

Composed by Lily Afshar

©1998 Lily Afshar. All Rights Reserved. Copyright assigned 1999 to Mel Bay Publications, Inc.

About the Author

Iranian born guitarist Lily Afshar, hailed by the *Washington Post* as "remarkable, impeccable," is head of the guitar program at the University of Memphis. Chosen as "Artistic Ambassador" for the United States Information Agency to Africa, she is the winner of the Tenth, Eleventh, and the Twelfth Annual "Premier Guitarist" awards respectively, awarded by the Memphis Chapter of the National Academy of Recording Arts and Sciences, Inc.

Winner of the Tennessee Arts Commission "Individual Artist Fellowship" Award in music and a National Endowment for the Arts Recording Award, Ms. Afshar was also a top prize winner in the Guitar Foundation of America competition, grand prize winner in the Aspen Music Festival guitar competition, first prize winner in both the Music Teachers' National Association and the American String Teachers' Association guitar competitions.

Lily Afshar was among the twelve international guitarists selected to play for Maestro Andrés Segovia in his master classes held at the University of Southern California at which time Maestro Segovia predicted that "she will be a beautiful celebrity." Ms. Afshar has released seven CD's and published "Essential Bach" with Mel Bay editions. For more information see http://lilyafshar.com.